SMALL MERCIES

poems by
Peter Huggins

Solomon & George Publishers
Auburn, Alabama

Copyright 2021
ALL RIGHTS RESERVED

1. Poetry

ISBN: 978-0-9986362-5-2

First Edition

Cover Image: Wordsworth's Dove Cottage

Cover Design by Saya Creative

Contents

I am thankful for small mercies.

Emerson, "Experience"

The Harpist Plays *Romeo and Juliet*

In Prokofiev's *Romeo and Juliet*
The dancers become the lovers they play.
I marvel at their ability to slough
Their age and inclination and assume

The role of that pair.
They glide together, unite,
Separate, and meld once more.
They whirl and spin but not for long.

These lovers must have each other to be
Who they must be. Then I play my part.
I pull my harp to me, run my hand
Along its curve, and pluck

Its strings which hum and vibrate.
In this pit and hall
These lovers are the music I play.
I play until the music and the body are one,

Until the music and the body are at rest.

Charlie Parker and the Cow

After he heard that livestock
Liked music, Charlie Parker
Drove to the country, jumped
The fence to a pasture and played
His saxophone. No crowd
At the Apollo heard what
He played. No horse appeared,
No sheep or goats. One lone cow

Wandered over and headed
For Charlie who played on.
Perhaps for the first time
In its life the cow decided
To join in: it riffed on moo
As Charlie played and played.

Wordsworth at Dove Cottage

Domesticity and too much noise
Drove me into the garden where
I could walk and compose, walk and compose.
Something about the light and air

Allowed me to find myself
As I found the world around me,
Each discovery a revelation
Of flower, water, fell, and tree

That took me into the heart of things.
It was beautiful to feel
Nature working in me,
A harmony of being and purpose

In which I moved and breathed and loved,
The life of one, the life of all
Here in this place and far beyond,
England and everywhere linked by

Deep clouds, falling water, light.
Here will I step on stones, follow
The work of bees, insects, flowers.
Here will I grow old, ripe as a pear.

Edmund Hillary and the Bees

He robbed bees like he robbed mountains:
On the principle he would get stung
Or fall except he didn't fall.

I attribute this feat
To eating honey and pollen,
To sticking his arms in hives,

Knowing he would get stung,
But doing it anyway,
The comb and honey worth
The price of twelve or a hundred stings.

Prepared for ascent, he summited
Everest, breaths like bee stings,
Red and white clover far below.

Box

When I open it,
It flowers.

Its nectar
Provides drink
After drink.

It does not
Dry up.

I return
To it
Again and again.

I call it
A wonder.

I do not lose
A single
Drop.

Butterflies

I love to see them rise
Their bodies
The color of light

They are souls
They are pilgrims
They could be witches

They are love
They are good luck
They are nature's lottery

I will never give up on them
They bring us dreams
They wake us up

Greece

Goat cheese.
Olive oil.
Wine.
The wine-dark sea.
Fish.
Ouzo.
Ruin.

Pomegranate Seeds

I love to eat
Pomegranate seeds.
They are what Hades,

Lord of the dead,
Gave to Persephone,
Ensuring her return.

Her mother gave
The gift of winter,
Clean and bitter

As a chrysanthemum,
Flower of the soul
Of which I am in awe.

The Bridge of Glass

Not the bridge of sighs in Venice
Under which lovers kiss at sunset,
The bridge of glass in Tacoma.
Above us pieces of Chihuly
Glitter and wave like kelp.

Like salmon, we emerge
From the chute to our home stream
In the House of Glass.
We birth our young in shapes
That are weird and free.

My Girlfriend Ate Salmon

I've seen the photo hundreds of times,
The famous last frame of the film:
Butch and Sundance storm out of the house,
Guns blazing, Bolivian soldiers
About to shoot them. Etta's gone,
Not wanting to stick around
For the inevitable finish.

The photo drew me to the film,
Which I watched to the end.
The music rose and the credits rolled,
But in my mind a salmon leaped
Upstream, birthed its young and died,
An image I now let go in this
Thirty-ninth straight day of rain.

There Be Treasure

Forty miles from Tampa,
We dropped anchor
In a light chop and started fishing.

When the swells hit us,
The boat flipped and into the water
We went. I climbed onto the keel,

Fred and Buddy raised
Their hands and floated away.
Big guys they were,

Strong, too, lineman types.
Hour after hour I held on,
Through the long night,

Into the next day
Until, past noon as I judged,
The cutter found me.

Maybe Fred and Buddy will form
A ghost crew on a ghost ship,
Sail the old Spanish Main,

Chase gold-laden galleons
That ride off the map,
For there be treasure, there be monsters.

Finding Bones

I am always finding bones
In the woods behind my house,
Mosasaurs or zeuglodons,
A paleontologist's dream.

The neighborhood children use
These woods for games and exploration.
I see them running past.
Sometimes they stop and share

My fascination with bones
As I unearth eighty
Million years of the past
From one bit of Alabama.

The older children
Avert their eyes.
They trudge down the path
To the fifty-foot drop

Or to the hut they built
From odd pieces of lumber
Or fallen wood they picked up
After last week's storm.

I am not prepared then
For what comes from my dig
Early one morning—
Love cries, soft moans, a giggle.

As you might imagine,
My appearance startles them.
They stop in mid-stroke, uncouple,
Grab their clothes, and run.

The wonder of that act
Leaves an afterglow
In the burned air
That surrounds this site.

I get my brushes and brooms.
I dig down
Toward mythic discovery,
Femur, thigh, rib,

Claw, skull, and spine.
I swear I'll piece together
One whole skeleton
Before I am through.

Small Mercies

Blueberries from bushes in my backyard,
Herbs from my own garden.

The smell of lavender when I walk
Around the corner and down the path.

The crunch of gravel, the call of geese,
The fall of water, the horn at noon.

Red birds in the flowering cherries,
Barn swallows against a darkening sky.

The brush of memory: the girl I thought
I had to marry, the woman I did.

Marriage

They put it on, like a suit
Or dress. It fits so well
They decide to keep it on,
Even while they sleep.

Fortune Cookie

My wife and I leave
The Mandarin House
Feeling happy and full.

We walk to our car
Behind the restaurant
As two old women

Scrounge for food
In the dumpster.
The manager yells

At them to leave.
We have nothing
To give them,

No egg roll or soup,
No sesame chicken,
No shrimp and broccoli.

The manager drives off.
The women hunt for food.
We take them inside,

Buy them dinner.
They are the happiness
The cookie predicted.

The Man with Talking Hands

At the Alabama School for the Blind,
He puts his hands

To his face and talks to them.
He tells them to see for him.

He wants to walk in fields
Of red clover, follow the rainbow's

Arc after summer rain,
Take a delta sky

Into him and feel clean.
His hands understand.

They know history's weight,
They won't let him down.

When he uncovers his face,
His hands tell him where to go.

Indian Food

My father lost
His taste for chicken tandoori
When his graduate student,
Mr. V. N. Naipoor, sent
His best greetings from the Cardiac
Care Unit at University Hospital.

My father watched
The heart monitor rise and fall.
Naipoor suffered
No ill effects but left
Academics for a corporate
Career with Dow.

In the Skilled Care Unit,
My father ordered
Chicken wings and described
The biochemistry of loss
As pine trees snapped and fell
In a sudden summer storm.

In Louisiana, Meditating on Sisyphus and Marcus Aurelius

After the storm the wood floors buckled,
The walls sagged, a ghostly line
Of the water's presence, the downstairs
A jumble of muck and debris,
The plumbing and electrical shot.
I thought of Sisyphus and Marcus Aurelius.
Nature defeats us all, he said.

We could, of course, walk away from this,
Leave the house as is.
Better to eat some bread and cheese,
A few oysters, drink some beer,
Start over. In a flat time
We live on borrowed land. We build
A little higher, we push the rock uphill.

Listening to the Volcano

Some take no comfort
In the return
Of wolves to Yellowstone.

Some would shoot them
On sight, finding them
A luxury they can't afford.

Let them be, I say.
Let them roam. We need
Their point of view,

Their voices to which
We listen as we gather
Around the communal fire.

Suicide Is the Single Stalk

For some it's thorns on blackened
Bushes on which no butterflies
Light, no birds sing.
For others it might be petals
On roses, mums, carnations.
You pick them, you decide.

But I say it's the stalk
That can't crack the ground,
The blade that can't push through,
The lover that climbs the mountain,
Refuses to hear the chimes,
Falls into silence.

Winter Is Not a Desolation

Winter is not a desolation,
An end, it is a beginning.

It is a setting out,
A facing of all that is.

It is a giving in,
But not a giving up.

It is a living through
As well as a living in.

It is an anticipation.
It is the voice that holds

Our attention the longest.
It is a stillness, a consolation.

Oaks
    after Machado

In my high office
I see some bare oaks
On a black road.

Buses chug a hill
Distant as the moon.
Surely you remember?

The blasts of February
Howl through the cherry trees.
I don't sleep and I don't dream.

Dorothy, First Wife of William Bradford

I told William I did not want to go.
He told me I must, it was my duty.
He bade me remember Moses' wife,
Who made no such complaint.
I therefore acceded to his wishes.
However, I did not fancy this voyage
To a savage wilderness that bore,
Despite William's protestations,
So bleak a prospect as we approached it.
Did I fall in Provincetown Harbor
On accident? Let me just say
I was not pushed. Consider William
Who, in his account of Plymouth Plantation,
Relates the story of the "lustie yonge man"
That survived a fall by holding on
To the ship's rigging. This man went on,
William says, to become a profitable member
In church and in commonwealth.
Consider further that William does not
Tell one story about me.
I was not worthy even of mention.

Makeover

In Dana Schutz's *Devourer*
The woman in the painting
Takes the next step
In radical weight loss.

She is not anorexic, bulimic,
Narcissistic, or disturbed.
The woman eats herself.
Mouth wide open, she begins

With hands and arms.
Feet, legs, and thighs follow,
Then pubis, core, and breasts.
She stops at nothing,

The rapidity with which
She goes astonishing.
She eats shoulders,
Neck, and face, mouth last.

Now she can begin again.
Now she can make herself
Into whatever she wants.
She is her own material.

The Wall

At the wall
I search for names,
Paul from high school,

David and Scott from college.
I find Paul, dead at 21.
He wanted to be a fireman,

Save lives, work the engine,
Get the people out.
Nothing of that life remains.

Scott and David elude me.
Career guys, perhaps they are safe,
Enjoying their retirement

In Florida or Arizona.
I do not find Elizabeth,
She is just missing,

A blur in memory.
I square my shoulders,
Move away

From the wall, and say
Their names,
I say each of their names.

Nietzsche at Sorrento

Italy came as a revelation
After the austerity
Of Basle and the denial
Of Schopenhauer.
He laughed aloud from sheer joy,
Wrote Malwida von Meysenburg,
His hostess at the villa.
He declaimed Goethe, Montaigne,
Stendahl, Plato, and Herodotus
To all the other guests.
A view of the Bay of Naples,
Mount Vesuvius, and Ischia
Lit up the living room.
Warm, orange-scented air
Drifted up the terrace.

No mountain ice here, no cold.
He swam in the Mediterranean,
Ate food cooked in olive oil,
Shed being old though he was
Just thirty-two. He chose life,
He didn't avoid pain
As Schopenhauer had advised,
He beheld himself on the path
To fulfillment. Years later,
Stunned because he was the first
Decent human, he embraced a horse
In the streets of Turin
As his one true and only love.

Popeye and the E. Coli Outbreak

Oh, Popeye, you ate one too many bags
Of spinach and the E. coli got you,
Not Bluto or a shark after Olive.

I see you laid out in an open casket,
Your best muscle shirt and sailor hat on,
Your big jaw and those classic

Beefy forearms still.
Bluto puts a can of spinach on your chest.
Rest in peace, he growls.

When Olive reaches for the can,
A whiff of her scent, fruity, floral,
Passes into your nose and you stir,

Sit up, and down the spinach
With your patented gulp. Bluto slinks
Away to figure out his next move.

Olive swoons. You catch her,
Murmur *Olive, oh, Olive,*
But Olive lets you have it

With an uppercut to your jaw,
Then stomps out. Everything is back
To normal. The comedy resumes.

Black and White Movies

I love them, those old
Black and white movies.
I could sit and watch all day.
You know them, too. We could
Round up the usual suspects,
The Philadelphia Story,
Citizen Kane, The Maltese Falcon,
To Kill a Mockingbird,
Or maybe *Ninotchka, High Noon,*
All Quiet on the Western Front,
Whatever you want.

Let's go with *Casablanca.*
Rick will always send Elsa
Away with Victor on the Lisbon
Plane, will always shoot
Nazi Major Strasser,
Will always walk with Louis
On the wet tarmac, will
Always lie low in Brazzaville.
Let's settle in, enjoy
The movie, just you and me,
Then take the bus out of here.

Red Cowboy Boots

The best boots
On shelves taller
Than I was.
The red ones fit,
But I couldn't get them,
I was the child
Who couldn't walk,
A complete
Failure as a human
Being, crawling around
On all fours,
So useless I couldn't
Drive a nail
Or frame a house.
Now I put on the boots,
Clump out of the store.
I am whole,
Human after all.

Natatorium

The Tulane Natatorium
Served the day camp
I attended at eleven.
I earned my Red Cross
Lifeguard certificate
Under its dome,
Swimming half a mile,
Treading water for five,
Ten, fifteen minutes,
Pulling a buddy
To safety with my best
Dog paddle stroke,
My eyes burning
From too much chlorine.

Baseball after lunch,
Whitey pitching,
A curve and fastball
Hard to hit,
Me at short or center.
We played all afternoon,
Never losing, not even
The counselors could beat us.
A ball over my head,
But I caught it,
I caught it.

No More Marx

No more Marx for me,
No more Nietzsche,

No more Kierkegaard and Sartre,
I'm done with that conversation.

Give me line and motivation,
Sound and character,

The word and labor
That belong to me.

Go ahead, break my heart.
Go ahead, do it.

The Heart of the Matter

Shelley's first wife drowned herself
After the poet abandoned her
For Mary Wollstonecraft.
When Shelley drowned while sailing,
Mary burned the body
Where it washed ashore—except
That Shelley's heart would not burn.
Mary wrapped the heart in silk.
She carried it around with her
For the rest of her life.

Reverend William Buckland,
The geologist and priest,
Ate Louis XIV's heart
More than a century
After Louis's death—I do
Not think the old king's heart
Would have been tender
Or much to eat.
Perhaps Buckland enjoyed it,
Though how he came by the heart,

How he knew it was Louis's
I do not know. I do know
That durian fruit,
A delicacy in Southeast Asia,
Bears the fragrance
Of a rotting corpse.
An acquired taste, I gather,
But no worse than Alfred Hitchcock's
Fear of the apparently
Innocuous, lowly egg.

Caribbean Cruise Line

I've looked all over the ship,
But can't find you.
If you've left this time,

I'll pack your clothes and shoes,
Give them away. I'll pitch
Your unused lipsticks,

Your eyeliner and Bare Essence,
Your tubes of body cream,
The polish for your nails,

Those endless boxes of tissue.
I'll gather strands of your hair
From the bathroom floor,

Tie them together with red ribbon,
Burn them in the fireplace
We seldom used.

The Atomic Kneedrop

These wrestlers glow
As they jump into the ring.
Even the Princess of Darkness
Shimmers in her hooded face.

When she stalks Southern Sue,
Sue doesn't have a prayer:
The Princess takes her
Down for the count.

Jungle Woman leaps
Into the ring and kneedrops
The dark Princess
Before she works

Her evil spell. Jungle Woman
Picks the Princess up, slams
Her to the mat and pins her
Before she can bridge out.

The crowd cheers and shouts
Jungle Woman! Jungle Woman!
Jungle Woman circles the ring.
Undisputed, she rules.

Red-Shouldered Hawk

I feel him before I see him
Circling in the sky.

When he spots prey,
He's a terror:

Eyes, wings, talons, beak are
One motion. The strike,

The rise, he's gone.
I wonder at what I saw.

Good-bye, Neil Armstrong

As usual, you slipped away
When no one was looking,
Leaving the press of people
Behind. You wanted
No shrine, no memorial
That people could visit,
Just those few words
On the moon.

I watched you land,
I watched you come home.
I remember 1969,
But I would not go back.
The world is what it is,
I am what I am.
They scattered your ashes
At sea, a Navy man to the last.

The Elegant Universe
after Brian Greene

A piece of string,
Curved space,
That's all it is really.

When I pluck this string,
Other strings answer,
A music of the eye,

A field of sound:
Extremely strange
The symmetry

Of this universe.

Three Women in Black

Three women in black walk down the stairs.
They have something to tell me.
Words run out of their mouths like ink.

I chase the words, which jump
Into my bag and hide
In one of its pockets.

When I look in my bag,
The words have turned into
A book in which I read

Three women in black walk down the stairs.
They have something to tell me.
I turn the pages faster and faster.

The pages click like the women's heels.
The women walk down the stairs.
Study us, they say.

I close the book and follow them.
I become wise.
The words pour out of me like ink.

Questions about Aristotle

Was Aristotle happy?
Did he have a pet?
Did he have a favorite food
Or drink? Did he enjoy going
To the theater? Who was
His favorite god and why?
Did he like the lyre?

Did he ever relax?
Did he like having Alexander
As a pupil? Did he treat
The young prince differently?
Harder on him than others?
Was he easy to talk to?
Did he like a good joke?

Cruzatte

Half-blind though he was,
Cruzatte knew he saw an elk.
It moved with a grace

No human could match.
He wanted it as much
For that as for the meat,

Hide, and bones.
Perhaps its sudden presence
Startled him and he thought

It was Blackfoot warriors
Come to kill more
Of the Corps of Discovery.

He raised his musket and fired.
When the smoke cleared,
He realized he'd shot

Captain Lewis in the thigh.
Lewis's leg soon mended.
No harm done, the feeling went

Among the Corps, though
Some said that Cruzatte was
Not only half-blind, but all crazy.

Ordway

Like the other sergeants,
Ordway kept a journal
Of the expedition.
He sold his journal for $300
To Captains Lewis and Clark,
Bought farmland near New Madrid,
Where the Mississippi turns
On itself, loops north.

When the earthquakes struck,
His land and house rippled
Worse than white water,
Worse than Pacific surf.
Wife dead, farm useless,
New Madrid a ghost town,
He died unremarked,
Forgotten, and lost.

Can Grande's Dottore

I did all that my lord
Mastino asked but I don't think
He'll do the same for me.

For poisoning Can Grande
My execution awaits.
Mastino forced me to help him

Murder Can Grande. He took
My wife and children,
Locked them up and said

They'd starve. What else
Could I do? Now they'll starve
Anyway and I'll lose

What remains of my life.
This is justice for Can Grande.
What justice for Mastino,

Flags flying, crowds cheering,
Safe on his throne? No comfort
In that, no comfort at all.

Cellini

Devils in Rome, devils
In the Colosseum.
The necromancers
Fabricate them out of the air,
Their low guttural speech
A second invasion and sack
Of Rome. You can believe
I call on all the saints
To protect me.
Those devils are nothing
To the ones in my dreams,
Eyeing me, marking me
As one of their own.
To compensate,
God gives me this halo
Of light around my head.

I see this halo at morning
When the grass
Is heavy and moist with dew.
The sun accepts me,
Treats me like an honest brother
Who gives what he promises.
I welcome those promises:
My imagination requires
Nothing to inflate them.
Doctor Faustus may meditate
On secret knowledge and occult
Power. I have within me
The hidden wisdom which seeks
No other as I perform
The daily task of purifying
Old objects, old emotions
Into new shapes, new devotions.

Root and Branch

In the hot August night
I walked Broadway,
Seeking relief.

Too young to drive, I hoped
To catch a breeze off the river,
Anything to cool me down.

I liked the clicking sound
My shoes made on the pavement.
I thought of boots on stone,

The prowling soldiers I'd seen
In last week's movie,
The Diary of Anne Frank.

My friend Chip told me
He must never imitate
The Nazis. I thought

I understood. I'd been
To his bar mitzvah, I'd been
A wanderer, a companion

To owls. In the moonlight
I balanced the grief and pain
Of the unspent lives around me.

My grievance was the world.
I walked on and on,
But never once in step.

Hair

We are the hair of millions
The hair of young girls
The hair of grandmothers
The hair of pregnant women
The hair of the newly married
The hair of the middle-aged
Brown hair and black hair
Red hair and blonde

We have value
Like the shoes
Like the gold fillings
Like the spectacles
Like the razors brushes combs
Whose hair they will
Never pass through
Never cut never brush again

Two Women

In the brothel
At Dachau
Two women survive

By finding
A bidet

Which in addition
To its other
Uses

Makes an excellent
Footwasher

Men's Room

In the men's room
At the Holocaust Museum
I stand in line,
Wait my turn.

The door shuts behind me.
Others crowd in.
The uniformed
Security officer

Patrols the sinks.
When I wash my hands,
The hissing water
Sounds like gas.

The hand towels
Going into the trash
Seem final
As the banging of the bin.

I rush out
Of the men's room.
Not today, I think,
Not today.

War Bird

The Aztecs made
The hummingbird their god
Of war who demanded

Human sacrifice to stave off
The last days, the world's end.
The hummingbird at my feeder

Is unwilling to share its bounty
With any other hummer
Even though it

Can't drink half
Of the feeder's nectar.
The hummer's a bully, you know.

It will attack and kill
Any hummer that approaches
The feeder. No wonder

The Aztecs thought
A dead warrior would be
Reincarnated as a hummingbird.

The Wild Geese

After a summer of loss,
I found myself out of sorts,
At odds and ends. First to go,
My mother, who wanted nothing
More than to go home and did.

Next, my brother-in-law
Who went out with a party
Loud as thunder,
Long as evening rain.
I'm in there, too, lost
In the Meniere's,

Not knowing if I'd come out
Again or what, the clarity
Of my vision such that I saw
Either in minute detail
Or in a sort of whirling myopia

That left me nauseated. Now,
The leaves fall and in the pasture,
On the pond over the ridge,
In the trees beyond the pond,
The wild geese return.
The wild geese! The wild geese!

An Eclipse of Birds
  for Martha, the last passenger pigeon

They covered the sky.
Audubon saw them,
An eclipse of birds
That outlasted the sun.

A century later,
In the Cincinnati Zoo,
Patrons threw sand at Martha
To make her move.

She refused—her wings
Drooped and she trembled.
Her taxidermied form
Remains along with

The Carolina parakeet,
Labrador duck, dodo,
Great auk and heath hen.
In the first five months

Of fighting in 1914,
A million soldiers died.
They covered the earth,
They fell from the sky.

Stroke

From my wife's hospital window
I see the choppers land,
One by one, on the helipad.
Patients on stretchers emerge,
Then are whisked away

To surgery. Just so my wife
Who arrived some days ago—
Or is it weeks now?
I feel the terror of unknowing,
The difficulty of taking

A step as if I were
Navigating a minefield
Without a map. But then
I'm through and I can breathe
Again and I throw up.

Later I wonder what all
The fuss was about.
The boredom takes over.
How will I make it
The next minute, the next hour,

The next day? This waiting's
A game that I'll never win,
But I keep playing.
A chopper coming in rouses me.
I am in the war again.

Boom Boom Ladies

You know them, you've seen them
Advertise fireworks on TV.
They swish and sway and perform
All sorts of antics. They throw
A football that explodes,
They shoot off exploding flowers,
They send up balloons that turn
Into red, white, and blue flags
On the Fourth of July.

Then they drop
Their antics and don
Camouflage gear. They shoot
Through the screen,
Shoot all that move
Before blowing themselves up
In one final display
That is nothing if not spectacular.

Last Day of the Cretaceous

On the last day of the Cretaceous
Wind stirred the palm fronds.
No grasses grew on plateaus,
In canyons, beside rivers.

The previous afternoon a thunderstorm
Cleared the air. A red sunset
Glowed and in the evening
Shooting stars forecast no doom.

Small furry mammals huddled
Together. Streams were full of fish.
Moonlight fell on sand dunes.
The Himalayas did not exist.

On the last day of the Cretaceous
T. Rex hunted Edmontosaurus
Across a floodplain and brought
Him down in a tangle of channels.

As T. Rex ate his prey,
A light flashed, no more than
A second or two, then the impact.
A comet large as Mount Everest,

Faster than a jet
Struck the coast off Yucatan:
Shock wave and fireball,
Tsunami on the Gulf coast,

Falling rock, burning forests,
Violent winds, settling dust,
Smoldering plants and animals,
A dark Earth, then heat,

Heat and acid rain.
After the impact no more T. Rex,
No more Edmontosaurus. After
The impact the world became the world.

Urn

It is blue
Blue as the Earth from space
Though a bit paler perhaps

It is made
Of earth and water shaped
By fire and given to air

It has serpents for handles
The heads point downward
To the copper table

On which the urn sits
The table a sort of chamber
From which the urn erupts

Sending its plumes of corkscrew
Willow wafting to the chandelier
Hanging from the coffered ceiling

I stand in the corner
Take a breath and wonder
That I could want more

Richard, Eating His First Oyster

I couldn't imagine it:
He'd never eaten an oyster.,
Much less shucked one, and yet
There he was, shucking away,
The shells piling up around him
As oyster, cracker, beer
Followed in succession,
Richard proficient as any barman
At the Acme Oyster House,
Serving up his dozens
To legions of admirers.

Just so I imagine Lucius,
A Roman serving
On Hadrian's Wall,
Thanking his friend Marcus
In Coria for the gift
Of oysters, which he ate
On his return from a mission
North of the wall,
A reminder of home
While stationed
At the edge of the world.

In Praise of Wiley E. Coyote

You may remember the many times
He fell off cliffs or dropped down
Chasms deeper than doom, signifiers

He'd failed in his pursuit of Road Runner.
The anvil always crashed on Wiley.
The cannon exploded in his face

Or shot him past when Road Runner
Bent over. The desert can be cruel.
You've got to admire Wiley's persistence,

His business acumen in getting
Those products from ACME placed
In all the cartoons. Now he's making

His most ambitious move yet:
He's taking ACME public, the IPO
Attractive to investors. He's going

To make a killing, and soon, you know,
He'll have the funds to buy up
New Mexico, Arizona, and perhaps

Southern California. Road Runner
Will have no place to hide and Wiley E.
Coyote can retire. Beep, beep, indeed.

On St. Charles Avenue, Waiting for the Parade

I don't remember which parade it was,
Only that I was cold.
Hungry, I ate a nickel bag
of hot, unshelled peanuts.
Still hungry, I ate pink
Cotton candy swirled around
A paper cone, airy sugar.
The parade started and the crowd
Pushed me back to the cast iron fence
Behind which stood my friend Lynn
Who watched on a raised platform
From the safety of her family's compound.

In their elegant costumes
The masked men on the floats threw
Beads and doubloons by the hundreds
To Lynn and her family.
I caught a few beads that fell
On the sidewalk, along with some
Doubloons, but I didn't keep them.
I gave them to a small boy
Who had cotton candy in his teeth.
I walked up St. Charles Avenue
Toward home. I didn't look back.

Raptor Show

At the Discovery Center
In Callaway Gardens
I sit in the outdoor amphitheater,

Waiting for the birds.
Eagle, turkey buzzard,
Red-tailed hawk

Come down from their perches.
When their trainer calls,
They shriek and feed.

An owl passes right over me.
I understand its point of view.
I fear for the mouse.

The Gods Are Burning

At Tecume the gods
Have been appeased
With blood
Of the Lambeyeque.
Men, women, and children
Flee. The pyramids burn.

The men of heaven ride on horseback.
They eat their god,
They sing to him,
They drink his blood.
The old gods burn.
Jaguar eats well.

Diomedes and the Horses

I invite all my guests
To come from their rooms
And join me for a feast.
After they eat and drink,

I show them my stables,
My white mares tethered with chains
To their bronze mangers,
Empty of grain or hay.

I tell my grooms to feed
The horses as my guests
Stay and watch.
They do not suspect

These horses eat flesh.
My grooms whip
And club my guests,
Throw them into the stalls.

Teeth and hooves extinguish
Those cries of loss,
Then that steady crunching
As my horses eat their fill.

I fear no laborer,
No dung cleaner, no slave.
I fear only these horses,
Red as the savage god.

Zeus Recalls His Animal Selves

I have been many animals,
Bull, swan, eagle.
I have been stone,
I have been golden rain.
Hera does not care
For my antics. These
Little loves of mine
Do not amuse her.
She always discovers them,
Then there's hell to pay.

I pity my lovers, wish
There was some other way.
Perhaps I should remain
Eagle, bull, or swan,
Run or fly
Away and never return.
To have no other thoughts
But food and sex
Sounds appealing
Though Hera says

That's all I think about
Anyway. She would bend
Everyone to her
Own will, own control.
This is what we do:
We battle, we struggle, we love.
I concede some points to her,
Insist on others myself,
Know she will never believe
Women get more pleasure than men.

Friendly Fire

Home on leave from the Navy,
You went hunting
With your father and grandfather
In northern New Mexico.
You strayed onto
The reservation and were stopped
By a native patrol
On a road you couldn't
Find again if you tried.
No hard words
Until your grandfather
Came roaring out of the back
Of your parked truck,
Warmed by the Jack
He'd been drinking,
The argument he'd had
With your dad.

Before he could go
For his gun, you pinned
His arm behind him,
Then handed the bottle
Of Jack to the patrol.
You wished them one hell
Of a great day. You put
Your grandfather
In the truck and left
Before you were coyote bait.
Your father and grandfather
Never spoke to each other
Again. You reupped:
The Army this time,
No tour too dangerous for you.

Hot Air Balloon

You didn't want to go
In that balloon but thought
You should. It was your fear,

You had to do it. You climbed
Aboard and began to rise,
Earth falling away,

Nothing above you
But the New Mexico sky,
That impossible blue.

When you looked down,
Earth seemed foreign,
Inhospitable, alien,

A place to fall.
Other balloons rose.
You felt less lonely, less

Like a crash victim.
You kept your eyes
On the other balloons.

You rose and fell with them,
Circled to where
You started, began again.

Acknowledgements

Thanks to the editors of the following publications in which these poems appeared, some in different versions:

Alabama: Views and Words: "Black and White Movies," "Red Cowboy Boots"

Apalachee Review: "The Bridge of Glass," "My Girlfriend Ate Salmon"

Between the Lines: "Dorothy, First Wife of William Bradford," "Fortune Cookie," "Listening to the Volcano"

Birmingham Arts Journal: "Oaks"

Bright Illuminations: "Box," "Butterflies," "Pomegranate Seeds"

Chinaberries & Crows: "Bones"

Epiphany: "No More Marx"

The Gulf Stream: Poems of the Gulf Coast: "Raptor Show," "There Be Treasure"

Hospital Drive: "Indian Food," "The Man with Talking Hands"

Kudzu House Quarterly: "Wordsworth at Dove Cottage"

Louisiana Literature: "The Elegant Universe," "War Bird," "Winter Is Not a Desolation"

No, Achilles: War Poetry: "The Wall"

The Old Red Kimono: "In Louisiana, Meditating on Sisyphus and Marcus Aurelius" Seems: "Men's Room"

Spillway: "Edmund Hillary and the Bees"

Terrain: "Greece"

*These Fragile Lilac*s: "Small Mercies"

Xavier Review: "Caribbean Cruise Line"

About the Author

Small Mercies is the seventh book of poems by Peter Huggins; his previous books of poems are *A Gift Of Air, Audubon's Engraver, South, Necessary Acts, Blue Angels,* and *Hard Facts.* Both *Audubon's Engraver* and *South* were shortlisted for the International Rubery Book Award for Poetry. Over 300 of his poems appear in more than 100 journals, magazines, and anthologies,

He has also published two picture books *Thibodeaux and the Fish,* and *Trosclair and the Alligator,* and a middle grade novel, *In the Company of Owls. Thibodeaux* received a starred review from *Publishers Weekly* while *Trosclair* has appeared on the PBS show *Between the Lions;* in addition, *Trosclair* received a Mom's Choice Award, was selected as a best book by CCBC *Choices* at the University of Wisconsin-Madison and by the Bank Street College of Education, and was a Benjamin Franklin Awad finalist.

Among his other awads and honors, Huggins has been a Tennessee Williams Scholar at the Sewanee Writers' Conferece and has received a Literature Fellowship in Poetry from the Alabama State Council on the Arts. He taught for thirty-one years in the English Department at Auburn University and is now retired.